HOBERT
does a
Tradeshow

a modern business fable

by
Paul Holland

Dedication:

*To my wife and best friend Rosie
and our three children.*

*Thanks for waiting
until I got home from the show.*

A Brief Forward:

I had a great deal of fun writing this little tome.
I hope you enjoy it.
I hope you get value from it.
I hope it makes you think.
I hope it sparks something that enriches your life,
both personal and professional.

As an aside, the illustrations (to make a minor point) are composed entirely of letters, numbers, punctuation marks, etc. After all, we don't think "in language". That is merely a vehicle to help us draw lines around an abstract concept and share it with someone else.

In the accompanying work, Hobert's Notebook you will find some of my thoughts on this amazing venue we inhabit "the tradeshow".

There is also an appendix of sample forms which are available for your personal use to assist your tradeshow efforts.

You can obtain a copy of these on MS Excel by emailing hobert@swgmarketing.com

And now without further adieu, our Hero...

Hobert McCray opened his eyes
and got out of bed after only three tries

for while he was sleeping,
without any warning
Sunday had quietly
become Monday morning.

He struggled with coffee
and toast and his tie
then ran out the door
without saying good-bye.

He arrived at the office,
sat down in his chair
turned on his computer
and suddenly there
looming over his desk a figure appeared.
Slowly raising his eyes, it was just as he feared...

"Good morning, McCray"

a voice boomed out like thunder

"Good morning, McReedy",

he responded, then wondered

why his usually haughty co-worker was swerving

to wish him good morning, cause it was unnerving.

McReedy shook hands and exerted some pressure

then smiled a smile that would shame all cats Cheshire.

"Good luck on your new assignment, McCray"
he chuckled quite dryly, and thank God went away.

McCray had heard nothing
about some new task, yet
there it lay in a packet
atop his in basket

a large three ring binder
with a Post-It note stuck
to its colorful face,
Hobert thought, just my luck...

You couldn't mistake the handwriting there,

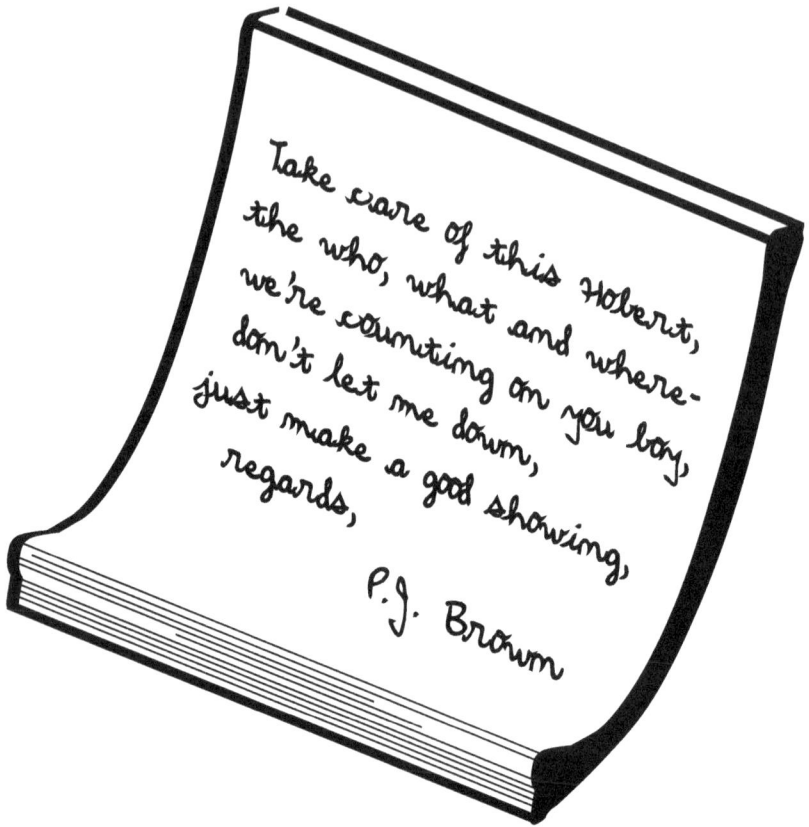

Take care of this Hobert,
the who, what and where-
we're counting on you boy,
don't let me down,
just make a good showing,
regards,

P.J. Brown

"Exhibitor Manual" the title proclaimed.

This couldn't be right, but there was his name.

What was Brown thinking, he didn't know

the very first thing about doing a trade show

Resigned to his fate, he then opened the book.
While he sipped at his latte, he started to look
at page after page of regulations and rules
about hiring labor if you had to use tools,
all about shipping, and booking hotel space,
sponsorships, specials and ads you could place,
renting data recorders, a table and chair set
and did you want padding installed with your carpet.

Did you need your booth vacuumed
and what about flowers,
seminars, workshops, exhibiting hours -

the room started spinning, where to begin
as he realized the trouble he'd just gotten in.

Well first things first, thought Hobert McCray
I had better go find our existing display.

According to notes in a file he found
the exhibit was stored here, deep underground
in a part of the warehouse that he didn't know
existed 'til now in the basement below.

Down staircases and hallways, floor after floor
into places he'd never ventured before.
Hopelessly lost after twisting and turning
Hobert said, "This isn't worth the salary I'm earning."

"Oh really",
a reply came
out of the gloom

Hobert turned and saw him
coming out of a room.

A grizzled old man
stood framed by a door
"Just what do you do that's worth so much more?"

Recovering from his initial surprise
Hobert more carefully chose his replies
"I'm the trade show manager, Hobert McCray
and I've come down here to inspect our display."

The old fellow snorted and broke into a smile
"Well, I haven't seen one of you folks in awhile.
You're the 13th "Show Manager" to locate this place.
Welcome my friend - to the totem pole's base".

Hobert's face telegraphed his shock and dismay
but old gent just said, "Oh, don't feel that way.
Most of your predecessors neglected to learn,
that in business respect always follows return."

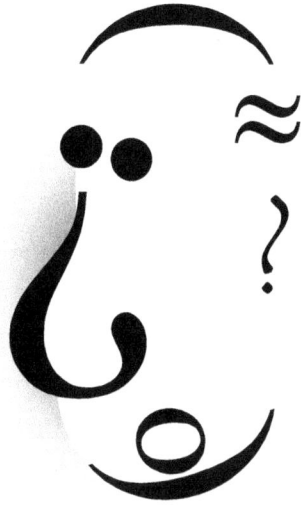

"I don't understand
what you're trying to say,
why even go
if tradeshows don't pay?"

"Oh, you can lose your shirt,
it's happened, he snorted
and often the payback
just goes unreported
but to it's a gross misstatement to say
that face-to-face marketing
doesn't pay it's own way.

Oh, forgive me, my manners – I always forget
My name is Biznak and I care for this asset."

Then the old fellow gave a look most unsettling
and said, "Please excuse me -
don't think I'm meddling-
are you experienced,
have you ever done shows?"

Hobert, thought for a second
and then said just…"No,

the reality is this got dropped in my lap and
now I'm expected to make this thing happen"

"Your story's not new, I'm sorry to say.
Two out of three folks get started that way
without knowledge or training,
learn as you go,
in the trade show business,
that's just status quo."

**"So this is it Hobert,
your really big chance.**

**You'll succeed
or you'll fail –
with an audience !"**

Biznak looked thoughtful and shook his gray head
"Relax, I can help you" the old fellow said.

"But your work is cut out, I've been there before -
got plenty of scars on the convention hall floor"

"Well I'm glad to hear it,
because just take a look."
Hobert reached in his bag and
produced the show book.

"Here's labor forms,
shipping forms,
a legal release...
This isn't a manual –
it's like
War and Peace."

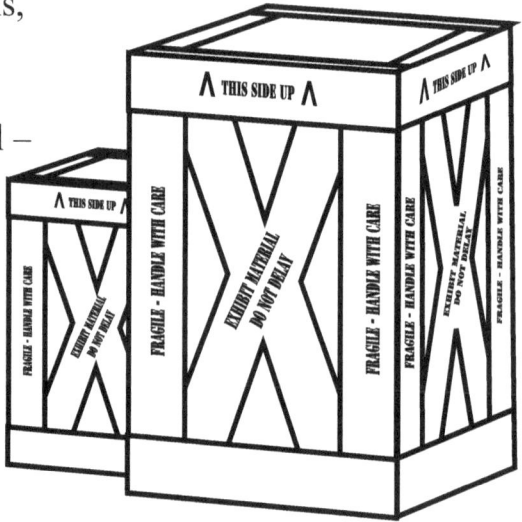

An unsympathetic Biznak stared back,
"Build a bridge, get over it
and let's stay on track.

Tradeshows you'll find aren't known for forgiveness
you're not ready on show day,
too bad - it's just business."

Now you didn't pick the show you're attending.
So options are limited, there's no sense pretending

    (by the way in case you wanted to ask,
     selecting the show is itself a big task).

As it is,
there is still the location to pick,
where you are in the hall
is part of the trick.

There are all kinds of practices,
                strategies,
                    theory

but it all boils down to just where you are really -
avoiding obstructions,
            dead-ends,
              the wrong hall

   if the people can't find you, get ready to fall.

Keep your eyes on the prize
and you'll see it through.
Remember, when this show succeeds...

                     ...so do you.

"Let's go through the book
and make up a list
of each service heading
so nothing gets missed.

Then make a notation
of each deadline date
so you don't miss
a discount by ordering late.

*On average you'll pay
more than thirty percent
in premiums for paperwork
that's late when it's sent."*

"In addition to copies
you keep here in your file
take another set with you",
Biznak said with a smile,
"to settle disputes
that arise on the show floor
as to just what you've ordered
and already paid for."

"The first thing to do is to set an objective.
From that vantage point, you now have perspective.
What is the purpose, the reason you're going?
That starts to determine just what you'll be showing."

"The number one reason folks go are for leads.
Finding our salespeople unfulfilled needs,
and they do a fine job, why just look in here
these are the leads they collected last year-
just where they left them, packed safely away
in one of the crates that holds the display.

Not a single one called, not a letter sent out
yet people will say that's what shows are about
we'll get to lead management, I'm not forgetting.
Right now, first things first - a little goal setting."

"So survey departments to find out what matters.
What is it they'd like served on big silver platters?
Marketing, finance and ask R & D,
sales and production,
what would they like to see?
Often their goals,
though diverse at the start
are achieved by the same path
(or leastways in part)."

"Once we've decided what we want to achieve,
we need to give thought
as to who will receive
the message we're sending,
so that they will hear
a compelling reason to stop,
loud and clear."

"Mixed in among all the noise and the traffic
is the person we need,
so what's their demographic?
Are they middle-aged, twenty or sixty by chance
with a background in science,
engineering or finance?"

"The message you're sending must reach the right ears,
attract the right eyes and draw them in here.
It won't matter how good your product is, really
if you're standing in Iceland and speaking Swahili.
Good messaging seeks to enhance and expand
the company's image, promote and help brand.
The message you're sending, to each attendee
both qualifies them and your company.
HERE'S OUR SOLUTION – does it fit your need -
then we should be talking,
oh yes, yes indeed !"

"Most of the people who walk through that door,
        (As a matter of fact about 3 out of 4)
already know who they are going to see.
They've known for a while, working proactively.

They've parceled out all of the time that they had.
If you aren't on the list - well, well that's too bad.

Before, during, after – promote that you're there
with answers they need, they must be aware."

Hey, who moved my cheese?

(on the subject of better mousetraps, I heard –
the fellow who said it had starved, at last word)

Said Hobert, "Here's a note about buying stuff
to hand out to folks and make sure there's enough.

Some mouse pads and pens and squeezee stress balls
tee shirts and hats and flashlights and all."

"And will all of this **STUFF**
at the end of the day
retain any worth as they give it away?

Will it build memories, buy us some info
or just fill up tote bags as they grab and they go.

Don't BUY stuff – **INVEST**
so when it's received
there's value in how it is used
and perceived.

Make it into a gift,
    make it part of a theme
        "take a demo and earn it",
           that could be our scheme...

but to simply pile this "stuff" in a lump, sir
save time and *shovel it right in the dumpster.*"

"But even before that, in advance of the show
you need to reach out to the people who'll go...

First from your database
(these names are the best)
who stopped last year,
because they've shown interest.

Canvas your sales force so no one is missed.
Talk to the show about renting their list
of pre-registrants, sort the segment we want *and*

Volia, now our market is there close at hand."

"So what do we tell them, these people we've found?
Determine the content, it's look, feel and sound.

What's in it for them when they stop at our stand
and is it consistent with our image and brand?"

"Think about themes, that'll help folks remember
what they saw in May until next December.

Consistency, clarity and timely arrival
are part of the secret to tradeshow survival.

The postcards, the faxes, your website and e-mail
a message that's mixed and muddied will fail !"

"In evolving our message,
also give thought
how it's employed
in the exhibit you've brought.

Divide what you must say
first into **three**
logical parts
with a clear hierarchy.

Who you are,
what you do
and your chief benefits

will attract and prequailfy –
look for good fits.

In under two seconds,
relate, plant a seed.
Show you have the answer
to their crying need."

The old fellow pulled out each drawing and spec
to show how the structure can influence traffic.

All that you do within this small space
contributes to help you meet face-to-face
or not, the point is to set forth a plan.
The message, the people and the form can
compliment each other and together it wins
or leave it to chance and take what happens.

Your exhibit does more than simply look nice.
Your graphics, structure and signage serve twice -
it attracts and promotes and it pre-qualifies
the attendees for you, and you in their eyes
and once their attention is locked on our page
the booth staff now has a chance to engage."

"Good training
will yield a return on investment
(that's one of the ways your money is best spent).

Selling at tradeshows is not quite the same
      as field sales
            or phone sales
                  as others may claim.

The cycle is different and so is the skill set
      and sometimes a *"sales guy"*
            is not your best bet.

          They're individuals,
       used to working their way

     but you need **TEAM** players
        to staff the display.

Ones who are comfortable engaging and greeting
hundreds of attendees walking the meeting.

Good questioners, who can hear and react
to needs and concerns and keep things on track,
focus on benefits and write it all down.

    That's the *real* reason
        that we came to town."

"Physically, mentally, booth staffing is grueling.
Invest in your people and then you'll be fueling
your tradeshow success, so make sure to reward 'em,
train them, include them –
in the past
folks ignored 'em."

"When I was a young man,
a long time ago,
we gave literature to anyone
there at a show.

Thousands of copies,
we'd go through in a flash

and most of it, unread
would wind up in the trash."

"Back then to "tell"
was the reason to go.

Today we exhibit
≈ in order to know ≈
more about clients to build up foundations
that can be the basis of business relations."

"Data are so many tidbits of fact...

but information's
the basis
on which we can act.

Without any context,
there's no way of knowing
where we have been
and where we are going.

Establish a format to collect every lead,
to quickly harvest the info we need,

electronic or paper,

the key to this task

is recording

the answers and

the questions

we ask."

When Biznak had finished, Hobert's head whirred
but he set about implementing
all he had heard.

Making his check lists,
building a time line,
reviewing the structure
and graphic design.
Meeting with sales, finance, IT,
Mar/Com, production and R&D.
Seeing their issues, setting objectives
based upon learning their needs and perspectives.

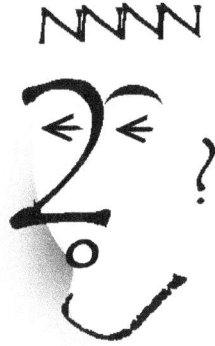

They sat down collectively, evolving a theme
in keeping with branding, then worked out a scheme
so that it was the backbone from which all would start
to insure the whole's greater than the sum of its parts.

Messaging, graphics, promotional pieces,
the script for the booth staff, new product releases,

the tchotchkes,
the print ads
all had to agree
to reinforce brand
and to build memory...

He spoke with IT
so that he would know
how to input the leads
direct from the show.

Cover letters were written,
avoiding delays
so show requests reached folks
in three to five days.

He set up a system to classify leads
according to size,
time frame and needs
and also established
a loop for feed back
so goals matched results
and they could keep track.
He gathered the staff
and he had them all trained
and he whistled and shouted
and called them by name...

(oops, sorry wrong poem).

He ordered and shipped
in plenty of time, too
avoiding late charges
that add cost without value.

He brought copies of everything
(and a roll of duct tape).

He was there when they laid the carpet and drape.

He supervised labor
to insure all was ready
and minimize OT
so his budget kept steady.

They made changes in layout
to encourage the flow
and positioned the staff
to get the most from the show.

He planned for contingencies –
any and all
and by expecting some stumbles
he avoided the falls.

He e-mailed the classified leads every day
back to the office while they were away
so that by the time
        they got back from the show
                fulfillment was packed up
                        and ready to go.

Leads and call sheets for sales also were packed
but with real information on which they could act.

                He filed reports to address all concerned
                within each department on all he had learned
                regarding the market, the competitive trends
                and emerging technologies shaping it's ends.

What's got them all talking, what's new and what's hot
in the original "chat room"? (and also what's not!)

New opportunities
to distribute their wares,
potential new partners
to increase market share,
the reports became part of his ROI file
along with the leads and the sales, but meanwhile...

        ...he saved press releases (it's free advertising),
                and made sure he checked
                if their stock price was rising.
                Impact study results and
                after show feedback, it
                was collected and collated
                and placed in the packet.

At the end of the day there were clear cut statistics
to support the show's place as a part in the mix.

And once again Hobert's life was less tense
thanks to good planning and old Biznak's guidance.

But since this a FABLE
I don't want you mislead
and no good deed goes unpunished it's said.

There's a little bit more to our storybook's close
about Hobert and friends,
and successful trade shows...

The following week Hobert found on his chair
materials for three more shows sitting there

but that was okay – he had been through it
while he might not know everything,

he knew he could do it.

While going for coffee
he leafed through a book,

He poured out a mug
and gave the danish a look...

when a voice most familiar
made him turn around
and found himself staring at

the boss,
P.J. Brown.

"Hobert, I wanted to talk to you son,
our last show exceeded all expectation

I've been watching your efforts,
they've been most impressive –

and in your next paycheck
I'll be more expressive.",

Then McCray noticed someone
cup in hand at the urn
Pouring his coffee
(as he started to burn)

...his rival McReedy, like a petulant child
stewed there in silence,

as Hobert just smiled

Hobert's Notebook

Companion notes to:
Hobert Does A Tradeshow
a modern business fable
by Paul Holland

Hobert's notebook

There are a number of books that I have seen on tradeshow and event marketing. Some have some excellent advice. Some don't. This could easily have become a textbook but that was not my purpose. The goal here is threefold:

1 – To provide some good information in a rapidly digestible format. Because no one has time anymore, unless we have to do something over and then we find the time (let's not go there).

2 – To be entertaining. That's why they put the cherry flavor in cough syrup, it goes down easier.

3 – To provoke thought. Challenging your program and makes it better. Take seminars, meet with your industry peers, and keep on reading the books... Obviously it helps to employ writers like myself, but more importantly this industry constantly changes.

All motion is relative, if it seems to be moving away maybe you're standing still.

2010 - the economy and evolution

"Adapt or perish, now as ever, is nature's inexorable imperative. "

H. G. Wells

Hobert predicts that the age of the behemoth tradeshow and its attendant megalith exhibitry is coming to a close, out of necessity. Our economic "ice age" is altering the landscape of this industry just as its glacial forebears did to the surface of our planet some 20,000 years ago.

Economic pressures compounded by growing concerns of energy shortages and the encroachment of technological advances in communications will result in a proliferation of smaller targeted, geographically dispersed shows but in order for this to occur, larger shows will be cannibalized in the process. For example, instead of the one week long show with 100,000 attendees – there will be 10 to 20 one or two day shows with 5,000 to 10,000 attendees.

Why? Less and less people have the time to leave their business for a week or more at a time. Financially, they will be looking closer to home to minimize travel cost. Faced with these constraints, they will venue shop for shows that more closely resemble their needs. The good news is that this will mean more shows but at a cost. This means the future of this industry will belong to the people and companies who can prove the most nimble. However for the exhibiting company, it can be a windfall if approached properly. Show selection will prove one of the single most critical skills of the exhibit and event manager because you will have the benefit of being able to target your client demographic much more efficiently.

As with all things; we can resist change but the odds of your long term survival are pretty bleak. We can continually try to adapt to change as we identify it, but then you are forever chasing a target that has already moved. **OR,** you can become an agent of change by developing the skill sets and programs best suited to survive. You do this by establishing a culture of change and in the process staying a step ahead.

Hobert says, "Change isn't bad, just different. Our inability to adapt to it is what makes it seem bad."

First, a few thoughts on the venue in general,

(and a few tips on how to capitalize on it)...

So, why go to tradeshows? Aren't they old hat? You bet they are and as the song goes, everything old is new again. With good cause, the roots of the tradeshow go back to the earliest civilization. Trade fairs and markets were more than just a means to buy and sell goods – they were the basic fabric of social interaction. Back then people were isolated by the lack of technology. Travel was difficult, dangerous and expensive. They needed market day to hear the news, see their neighbors and to find out what was going on in the world. Man is by nature a social animal. Guess what? The wheel has turned full circle and today the incredible advances in technology have buried us under a dearth of information without ever leaving our desks.

Now we find ourselves isolated again, but by an excess of technology. Go figure that one out.

That was then and this is...

There are two primary societal effects that have shaped the increasing success of trade show marketing. Both are based in the very essence of modern technology. As is the case with all things the benefits of these modern marvels that surround us come with a very hefty price tag.

The first of these two effects is speed. What we have sacrificed to obtain this is our sense of time itself. Everything around us continues its headlong acceleration and just as quickly, advances in such areas as computers and communications signal the death knell of waiting patiently for anything.

A scant fifty years ago, business ran on first class mail and carbon paper. The advent of increasingly affordable technologies changed all that. Suddenly, there was no longer the need to get to a phone; it was in your pocket. Documents were whisked half a world away in seconds. Mobile applications and the World Wide Web continue to reshape the fabric of business on almost a daily basis. In our personal lives everything from microwave ovens to DVRs have lead to the extinction of waiting. In the midst of this, the world turned upside down.

Forty years ago the pundits were predicting utopia. Young people entering college were advised to seek careers in leisure related fields because the workers of tomorrow will have so much time on their hands. Well, its tomorrow. How is it then that we work 60 and 70 hours a week, eat lunch at our desks and worry about how we'll ever find time to pick up our dry cleaning? The answer is that time has become an all-consuming obsession. Rather than freeing us, the need for speed has become an addiction. For the proof of this, we need look no farther than the fax machine. (Does anybody still fax?). Once a source of wonder, how many times have we all witnessed (or committed) acts of verbal or physical abuse on this mindless machine for delaying us in our headlong course. People wonder where road rage and air rage and Lord only knows what rage arrived from. Folks have a hard time containing themselves for 14 nanoseconds while a program boots up. Why should we think it odd that they blow a cork when the car in front of them doesn't begin moving spontaneously as the traffic light turns green?

The end result is that deferred gratification is a thing of the past. Immediacy is the watchword of the new millennium. *Time is the new currency and we all live below the poverty line.*

In response, the trade show is still a virtual time machine. Here is a format like the Internet that affords the opportunity to meet with clients and prospects from around the globe, evaluate competitors, recruit talent, introduce new products, research new trends, evaluate technologies and assemble field people in one

place within the span of a days, even hours –
BUT it is not virtual. It truly is "real time". No
other marketing venue provides such a degree of
concentration, face-to-face.

Is it any wonder that the number of shows has
increased (higher degree of specialization), the
average attendance per show has dropped (it is
no longer a family vacation) and it will continue
to do so, even faster?

After the catastrophic events of 9/11/2001,
technologies like web conferencing and video
conferencing and virtual tradeshows enjoyed a
surge in popularity, but they aren't new. They
have been around a while. If they were truly a
replacement for the traditional tradeshow
format, they would have already taken control.
Like the Internet itself, dot com has become dot
calm. As the landscape of technology
rebalanced, two things happened. The Internet
and its attendant mobile technologies have
demonstrated themselves as invaluable tools and
that they are just tools. The tradeshow continues
to survive and thrive because it is rooted in the
very nature of our being. Today mobile
applications and social networking are hot
properties. They too will stabilize at a level and
the marketing mix will once more reshuffle the
deck, but they won't throw out the other 51
cards.

The second key element to technologies' dark
side is desensitization. From a marketing

perspective the average American is bombarded by over 1500 messages a day. In the interest of expediency and sanity's salvation, we have learned to tune out this plethora of visual white noise. Print media, billboards, the web; simply watch an hour of television and you may be exposed to anywhere from 40 to 70 commercials. The real question is - how many do you see? In addition to the sheer volume; we have seen cyber-babies break dance, space duels at the speed of light and dinosaurs walk again.

What are you going to do to wow me now?

Like millions of others, I remember watching Super bowl XXXIV (primarily for the ads – Okay, I'm a marketing junkie). That "halftime" was a particularly interesting one because it was at the height of the dot com bubble. I was fascinated by the sweeps afterwards. When people were surveyed as to advertising content, the overwhelming response was "Yeah, there were a lot of dot com companies but I don't remember which ones". With production costs, each of those 30-second spots each came with a price tag in excess of $3MM. Ouch. It was not that the ads were not creative or well executed; they were (for the most part). In my humble opinion, they were simply too glib. Their message was shrouded, but the biggest problem was not transmission - it was reception. They failed to distinguish themselves from each other. They failed to establish any link with their audience. There was no emotion, no curiosity, and no involvement. It was like someone showing me photographs of their last vacation, they're pretty pictures but they don't mean much to me. As a result America left to get a sandwich.

Marketing and promotion can be divided into three distinct camps. The first is passive remote promotion. This includes traditional media such as mass mailing, television, print media, radio, etc. This is a shotgun approach. There is no personal contact. General demographics can used as a guide to medium and market selection <u>but there is no way to determine whether the target audience in a receptive frame of mind</u>. The answer has traditionally been to increase repetition to create brand awareness.

Voila, you are in a death spiral. The increased bombardment reinforces the self-imposed isolation. You turn up the noise and the customer tunes it DOWN AND OUT. After all, this is the age of communication overload.

The second alternative is active remote marketing where targeted contact is taking place. Methods such as telemarketing and venue faxing, e-mailing, pod casting, they are cost effective but limited in scope and can be seen as intrusive thereby creating an opposite effect. What's the solution, increase frequency? What's the reaction; more hang ups, more full wastebaskets, more pushing the delete key, more unsubscribes....does that sound familiar.

The most effective means is direct face-to-face marketing. This includes direct field sales (the most expense option) and exhibit marketing. Industry estimates put the cost of sales initiated through exhibit marketing at about 30% less than that of direct field sales. This shouldn't come as a surprise. It is interesting to note that when surveyed, 71% of trade show attendees either influenced or had final responsibility for purchasing decisions in their company and 88% these same people said that they had not seen a sales person within the last 12 months. Forget Stephen King, from a sales and marketing position if you're not reaching these individuals that's a recipe for terror. Sales people are reduced to the level of mere order takers. This is not conjecture. Recent surveys report as much as 70% of all purchases are buyer initiated.

At first glance, it would sound as if the fault lies with sales. Not so, nothing in fact could be farther from the truth. The problem is inherent in the nature of our society. This process victimizes sales too. They get buried under countless "leads" that are little better than a name and telephone number. Heck, they could get that from a phone book. On average, it takes 3.4 phone calls just to reach someone today. On a personal level, I might genuinely like a particular sales person, but I don't have time to talk about the fishing. In this era of time compression, sales people must be resources and problem solvers. Frankly if a sales person is calling on accounts when they don't have a problem – they become the problem.

Point – we need to see people, but only when we need to see them.

It is small wonder that the multi-billion dollar face-to-face exhibit marketing industry has grown consistently and will continue to grow. Not just in spite of technological advances but in part as a direct reaction to the pressures of iNfluence on eVerything in our lives.

In Nesbitt's landmark book "MegaTrends" and many others we see the cause and effect of these radical shifts in societal influences. It boils down to this - human society seeks balance. It MUST have it. So when a shift occurs, such as the Internet or TV or radio or printed text that alters the fabric of how we interact, society will seek a new balance.

Here is where it really gets crazy, because of the headlong acceleration of technology – the absence of equilibrium is the new equilibrium.

There is no universal best to reach any audience. In limiting our means of contact we are also walling off segments of our market. To quote Robert Frost, "Before I build a wall, I like to ask what I am walling in and walling out." Any good marketing program will take advantage of a total mix. In the same token, it would be foolhardy to assume that any mix that works well today will still be appropriate next year (or next month). Good programs always challenge the value each of its component parts are bringing to the table. The fact remains that the best way to reach any client is they way THEY want to be reached.

Given that we accept the clear benefits of face-to-face exhibit marketing; the question becomes not whether to use it but rather how to best capitalize on the opportunities that this medium affords?

Some of the most common reasons programs under perform are:

You are in the wrong place.

People tell me all the time that they are going to a show "because we'd be noticeably absent if we didn't". To which I say – at least you'd be noticed. Shows compete with each other just as companies do. If you are standing around at show "A" while your audience has moved on to show "B" – expect to be very, very lonely. It happens every day and people blame the show (rather than themselves).

First, know who your audience is. Make a list of your 10 best clients (notice I didn't say biggest clients). If these are our best fit, obviously these are the companies and individuals that we do best to target. What is it about these firms that contribute to our mutual benefit? With this list in place, what elements do we see in common? That's really what we want more of.

Before you write a check to show management, challenge the numbers to make certain that they are providing you with both the greatest number and concentration of attendees that meet your target demographic client profile for the least amount of money. Hey, we shop for fasteners and software and toilet paper to make sure that we are getting the best product for the best price, why should this be different just because it is a tradeshow?

How do you determine what shows to attend?

If time and budget permit, it's best to walk the show first but that is not often practical. First read the exhibitor prospectus (check to see if the numbers were independently audited, most shows are not). Of course I want to see historical data and the demographic splits but I'm also interested in two other things. The past exhibitor list; there may be companies I know in that list where I might call an associate and get some first hand feedback on the event. The second thing is less obvious. I want to take a look at how the show is reaching out to industry at large. Their promotion can be geared to two audiences – prospective attendees and potential exhibitors. As a rule, they may or may not be charging attendees but you know they make their money on the exhibitors. If that's where the lion share of promotion is taking place it should make you question a few things. At very least they are certainly more concerned with their profit picture than packing the aisles with prospects. It is also interesting to note which segment of attendees they are directing the majority of their attention. Is it being aimed at CEO's, middle management or end users? In shows that may serve more than one market, is the one I'm targeting getting its fair share of promotion?

The key in any show selection is simple. Ask the question, is this show the most cost-effective forum to reach my target audience?

Make a competitive profile on those shows serving your market. Check the Internet (including your competition's events page), network with other exhibitors, talk to media contacts, professional associations and talk to your clients. Where do they go???

After making a comprehensive list of likely shows, check the prospectus and references then make up a preliminary budget. Who is going to give the most time, in front of the largest concentration of my target audience for my money?

Then do it every year. Things change. To survive, you have too as well.

In the wake of 9/11/2001, companies saw the need to challenge their programs increase more than ever. The current economic climate is doing that again. I believe that we will see a dramatic rise in the number of regional shows and in more specialized venues. As this trend increases, the companies that do a good job of show selection will have an edge on the competition because high degree of pre-qualification these shows will permit.

Once they are committed to a show, people agonize over booth location.

There are a number of different theories and methods but the big thing to remember is that if they can't find you easily, they aren't going to spend time looking. Avoid distractions, dead-ends, remote, secondary or multiple halls, physical obstructions such as columns. Put yourself in the position of the attendee and look at the logical flow. Where can you expect traffic to be the highest? Where will you be most visible from those points? Be where people would expect to find you. Is there a technology pavilion or a country pavilion that you should consider?

If you want to succeed – you have to go where the customers will be. What a concept...

Who's driving this thing?

According to Aesop, "Familiarity breeds contempt". We do the same events, the same way over and over again and what happens? Tradeshow programs tend to be thrown on autopilot.

Parts are missing, services are ordered late, graphics are out-dated, the staff isn't trained (in fact, they aren't even aware of the show promotion), take the old literature, here are some stress ball with our logo from last year (logo's the wrong color but that's okay), is there any duct tape, it's just a regional show (only about 3000 attendees), what about an extension cord, do the lights work, just throw another draped table in, it'll be good enough…

Does this sound uncomfortably familiar? You aren't alone, but…

Name a time and a place where it doesn't matter how you appear to your customers. Then take it a step further, why would you invest your hard earned money to look bad.

The reality is that there is no neutral ground. If something does not contribute to your brand, it detracts from it. It serves only to distract and confuse the core issue. Our message becomes diffused. When we take an interest in something, it shows. When we really don't care about something, the same can be said.

For many customers and prospects this is the only face of your company they will see all year, the only voice they will hear. Yet how many times have you seen an exhibit that just needs a good cleaning or that hasn't changed since you first saw it 5 years ago? How many times have you seen an exhibit and not had a clue as to what the company did? Perhaps worst of all, how many times have you seen an inattentive booth staff just hanging around looking bored? Good heavens, if you aren't interested in your product or service – how can you expect a complete stranger to be?

The point is that the devil is in the details in this business. This is your brand. This is your image. This is your market, face-to-face. Whatever happens good or bad, they are going to see it. Success requires a centralized focus and control driven by the omnipresent need to build the brand.

Invest a little time:

Squeeze every drop you can out of a show... it doesn't cost anymore. Start building a network of other people in the venue such as other exhibitors, contractors, media, transport companies, etc. You never know when you may need a new supplier or other resource.

You may simply wish to compare notes on a particular show or exhibit hall you have never been to.

You may want to exchange lists with other exhibitors or look at other cooperative marketing ventures.

See salespeople, distributors or manufacturers reps in action before you align yourself with them.

Court press coverage, they are out there looking for stories.

It is all about people – with that in mind, leverage your presence everyway you can.

Lack of clearly defined goals:

In speaking with a client once, he described a wonderful promotional effort that he had seen at a recent show. He explained that the company in question was holding a daily drawing for golf clubs. Attendees had only to drop their business card into a large fish bowl to enter the drawing and as a result *"they had hundreds of leads"*.

After listening to this I asked my client if he had dropped his card into the fish bowl in question and was assured that he did.

Then I asked the fellow if he ever had any intention of purchasing the exhibitor's product or service… His answer was *"No"*.

I asked if he recalled the name of this company that had collected so many leads… again, *"No"*.

The reality of course was that the exhibiting company had gone to great expense to collect the names of people who wanted free golf clubs.

There is an old saying, when you set off with no particular destination in mind, you will invariably get there. Yet, it is surprising that many good managers fail to establish well-defined goals for their trade show program. When asked why they are attending a trade show 85% will wrinkle their brow and answer "to get leads". Okay…

How many? What's their target demographic profile? What's the yard stick by which we determine the quality of that lead? What are the secondary and tertiary objectives for the show?

In order to have a successful show; we have to define what constitutes success.

In setting goals, good practice utilizes the same basic formulas that are used to establish objectives in other areas. Begin by matching synergies between your show schedule and your business and marketing plan. Knowing that you have a new product roll out in August may have a profound effect on how you address a June show.

EXAMPLE: You are a biotech company. You have a product for the purification of DNA. You want to expand that business; however you know that you have a new product coming out soon for the purification of RNA. Researchers, companies, institutes that are opinion leaders and/or potential volume accounts in this area take on dramatic significance. Here are your best beta sites and most current promotional leads in a rapidly shifting market. You cannot neglect your core business. You cannot promote a product that isn't market ready but you can have as a secondary objective a tactical plan to position yourself to succeed when the product is good to go.

Once a field of objectives has been fixed, they must be prioritized and goals should pass the following litmus test.

1. Focused: Is the goal clearly defined in scope? Unless the objective is specifically and narrowly defined it is <u>not</u> a goal. IT'S ONLY A SUGGESTION. For example, one primary goal may be to gather leads. However, unless you define what constitutes one you have a recipe for wasting time, opportunity and money.

2. Quantifiable: Setting target levels up front does two things. They give you something to shoot for and provide immediate feedback to determine what is and what is not working. A goal might be > 30 leads per hour that meet all defined qualification criteria.

3. Realistic: Goals should be attainable with reasonable difficulty. Unrealistic goals are seen by the staffers as such and usually reduce performance. "Well, we can't achieve that number anyway so what's the point." Goals that are too easy are an all expenses paid trip.

4. Timely: Influences shift from show to show. Attendance, demographics, exhibit hours, competitive influences (there's another whole section on this one), etc. Goals need to be re-examined on a continuing basis to insure that they are

appropriate for that show. Which brings us to…

5. Feedback: Goal setting works best in this environment when opportunity is created to continually re-evaluate the process. The frenetic pace of the trade show floor demands that the trade show manager continually assess their position DURING THE SHOW. The window of opportunity closes too fast to delay. It is not enough to sit back and think you followed the recipe - you have to taste the stew while it's cooking.

Remember: A good goal is one that can be obtained with difficulty.

The Plan:

How many times have we heard the old saw - when you fail to plan, you plan to fail. This is never truer than within the trade show venue because it is such a powerful, compressed medium. It is akin to a marketing rocket, taking you dynamically farther and faster. That's wonderful when you are on target, but equally unforgiving of miscalculations.

Assume you have a $1MM budget for your big show, drayage, staffing, space rental, pre-show promotion, the whole nine yards. Exhibits are open for 32 hours spread over 4 exhibit days. Every second of show floor time is costing $9.26, that's $555.60 per minute, $108,000 an hour. Even a small show presence can cost thousands of dollars an hour. How far wrong can you afford to be?

For this reason careful planning, including the evolution of contingencies is crucial to minimizing risk and maximizing reward. Face-to-face exhibit marketing is a unique entity. What you don't know and plan for can hurt you, a lot. No one is an expert in all fields. If you need professional help, don't leave it to chance - get it. It is simply good business practice.

Within the confines of your plan it is imperative that you incorporate a meeting schedule to optimize internal communication for your booth staff team before, after and during the course of the show. Meeting in advance insures that all parties understand their responsibilities and roles. The show floor during exhibit hours is hardly the time to familiarize yourself with what your lead retrieval form looks like or what new promotional information was sent out to prospective attendees. Having brief meeting during the course of the show, immediately before or after the hall hours provides a vital feed back process to download information between staffers and to craft adjustments based on real time events. (Show me a coach that doesn't revisit his game plan at half time and I'll show you somebody who'll have to sell peanuts to get into the stadium next season!)

When the show ends, it isn't over. Take a look at how to expand the effect of the show through your post show marketing efforts.

Budget:

Trade shows are riddled with expenses, many of which can be mitigated through proper planning.

For example: floor services typically cost about 30% more when ordered at the show.

In the planning stage, establish a line-by-line budget (a sample is included in the appendix). This will provide three distinct benefits. It will help control costs, it will provide a double check for your time line and it will allow you to accurately gauge your return on investment. It is also good to note that rental as an option may be used to defer capital expense on accessories and structural needs.

Read your show book and get help if you have to, there is nothing wrong with that....

When magnetic strip card readers first came out, like most folks I said we already have our own card imprinter. Why do I want to spend an additional $200 for that? When I got to the show I found out why I wanted to spend that additional $200 on something like that. *There were no embossed cards, magnet strips only.* I was fortunate. As was my usual custom, I would always allot plenty of time on the front and back end of the show to insure that everything was going smoothly. When I found out this was the case, I was able to rent a reader (at a premium) at the show. However so many others had made the same assumption there were hundreds of exhibitors that had no means of data collection. Show services had brought enough machines for pre-orders plus twenty percent, not nearly enough. People were going into neighboring displays to swipe cards. It was mayhem. Whose fault was it? *It was mine.* I didn't read the fine print, because I'd done plenty of shows. Always have contingency money in your budget. As is the case in any time driven forum, <u>there will be problems</u> and you will need it.

The best budget advice I can give you is this: When you set out to trim money in your budget, before cutting ask – is this something that will be apparent or transparent to the attendees? Always look for ways to save money on things like freight, storage, install and dismantle (I&D) costs first.

It is doubtful that anyone will walk up during the show and say, "Wow, I'll bet this cost a lot to set up". They <u>will</u> notice the dog-eared and outdated graphics, the cracked laminate and the inattentive booth staff.

Don't spend money on tradeshows…

INVEST IN THEM

…and treat it as an investment. Look at the incremental value that different components of your program are bringing to the table. What is central to the core mission? What directly supports? What is just taking up space and what distracts and detracts from our objectives?

Because this is a time compressed forum we all have the tendency to fly by the seat of our pants and make changes as we go. This is premium, quality time in front of our clientele and we should treat it as such.

This is a process comprised of many tasks. People tend to take care of the details (for the most part) but often neglect to insure that the all the pieces form the complete picture at the end.

It doesn't matter if all the "pieces look great" when the big picture is incomplete or out of focus.

Economics:

Trade show economics are a unique animal. By far and away the majority of your cost is direct expense. It is vital to remember you also have an important component of capital investment as well.

Avoid the temptation of considering the purchase of your display, graphics, models and accessories as "another expense". Unless you plan on throwing them out after each use they should be viewed as what they are - an investment in your corporate image. Amortized across their typical life span, the materials usually constitute less than 10% of your actual budget.

Example: You spend $10,000 on a display. You go to 5 shows a year and in 5 years you discard the display completely in lieu of a new look. Your amortization of the original purchase (exempting associated costs of ownership such as storage and maintenance) is $400 per show. Given the prices charged at the exhibit food concessions, you could conceivably spend more for hot dogs and beer. When viewed from this perspective it becomes patently obvious that image is one of your best investments.

The most expensive display in the world is the one that nobody stops in.

Rather than fret over the cost to look good, consider the high price of looking bad. Oddly enough, the difference in out of pocket cost is often times not that great. This doesn't mean that just throwing money at your display will guarantee success. Quite the opposite, before building or modifying your display, consider sitting down with a design team experienced in the industry that will take the time to get inside your business to craft complete solutions.

Once you have the display, MAINTAIN IT. Your displays often pass through the hands of many field people. (Who may be more interested in getting out fast after the show than they are in making certain everything has been packed properly.)

Get in the habit of setting up and assaying your displays after they return from a show. This will enable you to find damage or loss immediately rather than on the eve of your next event. In addition, depending on your requirements, examine alternative options such as rental to meet goals or experiment with concepts prior to investing capital.

Remember:

Things like: Ingenuity, attention to detail, continuity, clarity, consistency, commitment, professionalism ...

These are the lovely intangibles don't get line items on the budget, but when you invest them in your program - you'll see the rewards.

Your Three Biggest Competitors:

When asked, good managers can rattle off the names and market positioning of their competitors with no trouble at all. However, in the hectic world of exhibit marketing they will probably overlook their most formidable adversaries - time, sensory overload and themselves. A company that manufactures pumps or provides precision grinding services might not view a software house as a competitor, until they get to the show and find themselves dwarfed by an imposing interactive exhibit. Suddenly they find that they have paid dearly for the privilege of being their neighbor's anteroom as the overflow crowd creates a physical impediment to their customers and potential customers.

In addition to the incredible cacophony of stimuli erupting on the trade show floor, exhibiting companies must often resist their own internal demons. How many times in walking an exhibition have you see companies attempting to display every single product that they have ever produced in a 10' x 10' space? In Business 101 we talk about the evolution of manufacturing to sales to marketing focus within companies. There are times when it seems that tradeshow exhibiting had an arrested childhood. Yes, it's tempting because we're so proud of our machine that *we just know everyone wants to see it*. The reality is that our prospects don't care about "the machine". Their only concern is the promise of what it will do for them. Nobody buys a lawnmower; they buy the promise of short grass. In this crazy sound byte society, less truly is more. At an average walking rate on the trade show floor it takes approximately 4 to 4 1/2 seconds to travel 10 feet. Get that key benefit in front of the client in as clear, as concise, as dramatic a method as possible and do it in less than 1 1/2 seconds. Use every tool in concert to make it happen- graphic, tag line, text, booth staff scripts, premiums, advertising, promotions, follow up mailings - never miss an opportunity to reinforce your brand and it's client perceived benefits. In order to do that you must be consistent. In order to be consistent you must be committed to this as a process.

I always felt that it was criminal to refer to this as event marketing. That infers there is a distinct beginning and end. That is only true of the exhibit hall hours. The show lasts as long as we make good use of it.

Position to Win:

Having fixed goals and distilled our message down, we need to engineer our delivery vehicle. The display form is a function of these elements viewed from the perspective of the target audience. Visibility, clarity of focus, traffic flow dynamics, workspace ergonomics, this is your branch office on the corner of Main and Progress.

Everything must be tailored to capitalize on the most expensive business real estate in the world ($25 per square foot for three days translates to about $3000 per square foot annualized). Imagine paying $15,000,000 a year for a 5000 sq. ft. office. How far wrong can you afford to be?

Personnel:

When surveyed, 98% of attendees said that their negative impressions of exhibiting companies were due directly to the booth staff. How many times have you walked a show floor and seen people, talking on their cell phones, reading a paper, eating lunch or just perched in their chairs having their own private conversations while the market passes them by.

Unfortunately the typical sales person cast into the role of booth staffer is often a terrible choice right off the bat. The very skills that make successful in selling are contrary to those needed in working a booth. That shouldn't shock anyone. The telemarketer requires a different skill set to succeed than does the field salesman calling on an OEM account – but it's all "selling". Why would we presume that seeing people in a time compressed forum would not need a different set of tools? Field sales people might see 6 to 8 people in a day; the booth staffer may see and interact with well over a hundred. Optimizing your people to meet the unique demands of the tradeshow exhibit staff is really a book unto itself. (Hmmm, do I smell a sequel here?) Physically and psychologically it is extremely grueling. *The basic personality traits and behavior of your people is key in selection.* I can teach someone how to engage a prospect, qualify them, solicit key information, reassure them that we can meet theirs needs, say goodbye and write it all down. That's just process, it's technique. Select people for what cannot be readily taught. Are they team players, energetic, flexible, personable, and outgoing? Do they meet people easily; are they comfortable in a crowd? These folks can be instilled with product knowledge, or taught open-ended questioning and listening skills. If you don't think it's hard to teach someone to smile warmly and genuinely you need only walk down the street and count how many you see.

Check out the ten commandments of staffing in the appendix...

Promotion:

Exhibitor magazine reported the results of a recent study of the habits of show attendees by Exhibit Surveys Incorporated. The report found that on average the typical attendee spends two days and a total of 8.8 hours viewing exhibits. During the course of this stay each will visit 20 exhibits, staying approximately 23 minutes in each one. The study deducts for time spent walking the floor, phone calls, bathroom break and meals.

The average tradeshow today numbers about 400 exhibitors.

Now couple this information with the survey results that say 75% of attendees arrive with their agenda already filled out.

In short if you aren't already on the dance card, the odds of you getting a spin around the floor aren't looking very good.

Back to square one:

Change the odds

- The actual event is just a part of the mix.
- Don't think of it stand-alone element, it is a GREAT excuse to get in front of your client base. Not just for 3 or 4 days but for two or three months – before during and after the fact. I always felt

that it bordered on criminal to call this "event marketing" when it reality it is a process.

The best way to reach the prospect is the way they want to be reached.

- Given your event program is one component of the mix. Every medium has it's own strengths and weaknesses. Expectations of return must be based upon that, but this is a perfect example of where the sum must be greater than it's parts or failure is imminent. This is one of the great inequities of marketing. Mixed messaging doesn't just fail to contribute – it diffuses, diminishes and derails the mission.

Branding requires four things – repetition, clarity, consistency and change.

- Repetition reinforces and insures that we are there when the audience is ready to hear what we have to say.
- Clarity – what is your promise of performance?
- Consistency builds trust; it's the anchor.
- Change attracts the eye, the ear and increases the likelihood that our message will rise above the noise factor.

We cannot promote effectively if we don't know who we are promoting to. What is our "ideal prospect" demographic profile? One of the best places to start is who came from leads at past shows. We know that they are obviously candidates to use our product or service and that they go to shows. By the way take time to promote to your existing client base prior to the show. They use your product or service currently, but at the show you can bet they will be "comparison shopping" you. What's the old saying "just ignore them, they'll go away".

In constructing the pre-show promotion list, the number one candidate to invite will come from "leads" from previous shows, after all they have pre-qualified themselves by displaying interest in us – it's only right we return the favor. Look into renting the show's pre-registration list (see if you can get your segment presorted), talk to other exhibitors you may know about sharing lists and don't forget to canvas your own sales force as to who their best prospects are. One of our goals is always to get sales behind this process, what better way to include them.

Remember, not all prospects are created equal. Based on immediacy, potential and need there may be sub-strategies crafted to reach different segments.

Again – before, during and after the event applies to everything we're talking about here!

Once we establish the list, the content of our message and the medium that will carry it to these prospects can be determined. For maximum effectiveness, there are two litmus tests that this should pass. First, does it increase memorability? Optimally, whether before, after or during the event, it should include the attendee, draw them in. Fire their curiosity, make them think, involve them, teach them a skill. It's much more than leaving a pile of pens for them to grab or sending them a post card.

We need to remember that we want them to remember – so we need to make very sure exactly what that impression is.

Second, what is the benefit to the audience <u>clearly stated from their perspective</u>? What's in it for them? Think of it in terms of our purchasing blocks of their time. What "currency" will make it worth their while? Or why should they bother?

Logistics:

Shipping, handling, storage and drayage represent a substantial component of the exhibit budget. There are numerous ways to conserve. Here are a few good ones:

If you have back-to-back shows in the same city or region, ask your carrier if they can hold your freight. Many carriers will offer this service at little or no charge for short periods. If you are considering this it is important to remember that warehouses will not store blanket wrapped freight. In addition, there will not be any opportunity to inspect for loss or breakage on other than the show floor. For that reason, make certain that you pay extra attention during the pack down at the first show. Just as an aside, it is always good practice to stage and inspect your exhibit before shipping to show. It costs far less to repair here than it will on the convention hall floor.

Is there a local capability as a resource that may have been overlooked for assistance in storage, manpower or business services? Sources may include wholly owned offices or warehouses, manufacturer's representatives, distributors, even good customers. Actions as simple as receiving goods or having room sufficient to allow a vehicle to be parked can have value.

Remember, last in, first out. When loading the shipment, make certain that all material packs in reverse order. Assembled accessories such as tables and chairs are packed first. The pad and carpet are loaded last so they will be the first items removed. This will help save on wait time and help in controlling I & D costs. Make sure that you get proof of delivery on everything!!!

All shipments are not the same. Large amounts of collateral material such as literature (by the way 67% of attendees surveyed said that they would rather have it mailed – see the section on promotion) or promotional giveaways may be leaving with your shipment but finding it's way into new homes. Leave additional sales materials, demos, etc. at a regional office where it can be put to good use. If you have been exhibiting equipment, you may wish to sell it at a discount to a local customer or distributor. I have even encouraged some clients to donate larger product to local charities rather than pay to ship it back. They can take a full tax write off and get some nice public relations mileage. A larger display may be broken down into smaller configurations and dropped shipped to other secondary shows. Your outbound drayage invoices and any interim storage invoices should be amended to reflect this. Often people will forget and the original paperwork still reflects the higher piece count and total weight. Make arrangements for this in advance by estimating how many cartons will not be returning. Make all arrangements in advance with the carrier to avoid incorrect billing.

There may be times when it makes sense to pay a little more in shipping to decrease overall expenses. For example, a piece of exhibit material that would be costly to assemble on the show floor may be shipped intact for less than the cost of show labor to put it together.

Market Window:

In addition to being an exhibitor, remember that you are also an attendee. Take full advantage of that fact. One of the opportunities often missed, particularly by individuals new to the exhibit marketing arena is to gather competitive insights. Prior to the show, take time to map out the locations of those exhibitors that you wish to see either for competitive analysis or horizontal marketing purposes. Don't limit your opportunity to a mad dash to collect sales literature. Your marketing review on the floor should be focused in three areas:

The first area is at the direct competitor level. Here we talk about the five "P's", presence, promotion, product, presentation and people.

Take time to evaluate each competitor's presence. Evaluate lighting, graphics, design, etc. Do they possess a strong show presence? If so, how is this achieved? It is not a function of size. A lack luster, poorly staffed island makes a statement. It may not be what they wanted to say, but it makes a statement. A great deal can be said about their selection of design as a reflection of their corporate culture and the relative significance that they fix to a particular market.

Are they projecting corporate stability and strength or cutting edge technology? Are they creating an aura of comfort and relationship or fast paced responsiveness?

What have these companies done prior to the show to insure success? Surveys indicate that 75% of attendees arrive with an agenda prior to walking in those doors. This is not a fact that should shock anyone. Before spending several days out of the office and logging thousands of dollars on your expense account you want to make certain you get to see your "short list" at the show, don't you?

Review staff performance. How are visitors greeted? Exactly how is technical information provided (do they use technical staff, salespeople or presenters)? Is their exhibit over- or under-staffed?

Compare products and services. What products are competitors discussing? Are they focusing on a specific service, new technology or specific advantage? How does this compare to your own?

Analyze traffic activity. Compare giveaways, incentives, direct mail, contests, etc. to determine their apparent effectiveness.

Complete an overall comparison. What are competitors doing better or worse than your company? Why?

In addition, see what's new (and what's not). Are there any emerging companies, products or trends that are opening or closing your window of opportunity? While looking to see what competes with you, take time to see what may complement you. Are there any synergies with other companies or individuals as partners, alliances, investors or hires?

The Internet, et al…

In Nesbitt's book Megatrends; he spoke of the innate tendency of the human animal to build counter-cultural movements. The sociological equivalent of for every action there is an equal and opposite reaction. He correctly predicted that the reaction to the concept of the global village would be the rise of ethnocentric defense postures. A natural order to defend against the gradual dilution of established identities.

The same logic can be very readily applied in the case of trade show marketing. The advent of the Internet had pundits predicting the demise of the trade show. We would replace such events with the "Virtual Show". The traditional display would be replaced by one conjured from the ether. Plywood, laminate and fabric would simply be a mass of electrons skillfully placed by the graphic artist's palate.

Surprise (or not), quite the opposite occurred. The reasoning is simple. The information super highway is after all merely another tool for the dissemination of data, not a monopoly on it. In fact, as it and the crushing demands of our time-deprived society have diminished other forms of direct personal contact, the trade show has flourished. It makes perfect sense. The trade show compresses time, permitting direct face-to-face contact with customers, employees, representatives, competitors, and potential hires within the span of hours.

Considering that the global chat room is by far the most popular venue on the web what could be more natural? There's nothing virtual about a tradeshow - it's the real McCoy chat room.

Does this mean we should pull the plug on our servers? Of course not - in fact, there is an ideal complementarily that exists between the two media. We can readily (and economically) expand and promote our show presence on our websites, through mass e-mailing (make sure they opt in) and other emerging mass communication technologies. We can post live shots from the floor during the show and continue to promote in the electronic ether afterward. That just increases the likelihood that our target attendees will be reached. It artificially expands the hours of the show and the exhibit is an excellent forum to promote our web presence to increase traffic.

One of the big pushes is for web conferencing and teleconferencing. It has its place, but it has been around for years in various forms. It will enjoy its niche (in part because of the Internet's economies) but it is still the low calorie, caffeine-free substitute. We are social beings. We need to actually see each other.

High Tech + High Touch = Balance

ROI

People should stop spending money on tradeshows; and start investing it. Demand a return and accept nothing less. Everything we do in business is because we are more profitable with it than without it (at least that's the theory). This is not meant as commentary on the social responsibilities of business management.

At its most fundamental level - in the immortal words of President Calvin Coolidge, "The business of business is business". Consequently, if something is not providing a return a whether it's a show, a promotion, an ad campaign – challenge it. Set benchmarks to gauge your progress toward goals along the way. Not just for lead to sale conversion ratios, but for the total contribution of the program to the health and profitability of the organization. What did the new product introduction do to our stock price? What new trends or emerging technologies should our R & D people be aware of? Sadly, the tradeshow has long been relegated to the status of a "necessary evil" in business, even among large companies. For that reason, I say shame on us – the tradeshow managers. In order to succeed, we need to solicit cooperation from other departments and support from upper management. That will only occur when we can demonstrate "what's in it for them".

Follow leads, cradle to grave. When they go out to sales, it should be with a standardized feedback form that accompanies them. Have standardized formats for competitive reviews, reach and impact studies, strategic technology assessments and when these are reported also include in your file their relative commercial value. When you have press releases published in conjunction with a show, report the equivalent commercial value. If you sign up a new distributor, provide projections with regard to projected contribution to share and revenue.

Success follows success. If you don't champion the benefits that your program brings to the table in real terms, you will never gain the respect and support you are due. *(Check out Hobert's appendix… you know no matter how often I say that that just never sounds right)*

Lead and they will follow:

I purposely left the subject of leads until last, because it is what most people think of first. On average about 80% of leads are never followed up on. There are two reasons. The first is that they were never a lead to begin with and the second was that there was no mechanism in place to make it happen.

Many years ago I went to tradeshows to give out information, today I go to get information. Have a lead retrieval form, either paper or electronic, but the point is that it must facilitate the collection of information in a standardized format. It also acts as a prompt so that the staff remembers to ask key points.

The test of a good lead is that it should be so complete it seems like our conversation never really ended; it was just momentarily interrupted.

Have your mechanism in place to provide fulfillment before you leave for the show. I guarantee that you will be too busy to do it as soon as you return. Have templates ready for snail mail, e-mail, telemarketing scripts, etc. Make sure that printed material is identified on the outside of the envelope "thanks for stopping at our booth..." to differentiate it from other unsolicited mail. After all, the point is the relationship that we hope to grow from the encounter.

Good fulfillment should land on the prospect's desk 3 – 5 days after the show ends. That insures that the have time to sift through "the pile" and address immediate distractions before your material arrives, but their experience at the show will still be fresh in their memory.

Why retreat only to begin again weeks or months later from an inferior position? Fulfillment must be timely and accurate. Have your feedback mechanism to follow up through your sales network to gauge the relative success of the overall program.

ALWAYS, ALWAYS, ALWAYS get the prospect to confirm their contact data before they leave the booth. On average 30% of attendee badges contain errors such as wrong or incomplete addresses and misspelled names.

If they don't hear from you, they won't blame faulty data; they'll just think you don't want their business

Hobert's Appendix

(that just sounds so wrong...)

To request all of these forms
on MS Excel Spreadsheets
email:
Hobert@swgmarketing.com

These forms are provided for your personal use only.

The 10 Commandments of Booth Staffing:

You need to be the type of person that encourages contact; smile, be enthusiastic, up beat, warm and personable (without being over bearing). More than 80% of what you communicate is non-verbal.

Know the product stone cold. Don't get sucked into a three hour quiz, but you cannot stumble over answers.

Take care of yourself. Staffing is grueling. Get rest, eat sensibly, avoid excesses. Take breaks <u>away from the booth</u> to recharge.

Be on time, your fellow booth staff depend on you so that they can recharge too.

Be a team player. Communicate and practice selling skills with the other staffers. Meet often and stay in tune with the entire process.

Dress comfortably and appropriately. Be constantly aware of personal hygiene issues. It is all part of the image you convey.

The only thing that should be consumed while in the exhibit <u>is air</u>.

We are there for information. Ask open-ended questions, listen to responses and record it in an approved format.

Resist the temptation to sell. Speak to key benefits - from the attendee's perspective (3 maximum). Remember the average attendee visit is about 15 minutes, just enough time to engage, qualify, respond to their needs and record the information. At most shows, the "Close" is just permission to take the next step.

People came all this way, spent their time and money just to meet with you for a few minutes. Be attentive and helpful. You cannot do that while talking on your cell phone, collapsed in a chair or polishing off that last barbecued rib. You are your company's ambassador to the world. Act the part and not just in the booth.

Staffer Work Roster

Install:

TIME WINDOW:

Dismantle:

TIME WINDOW:

Contractor:
Address:
Tele:
Fax:
Cell:

Freight carrier:
Address:
Tele:
Fax:
Cell:
Pro # Inbound:

Forwarding:

Special Instructions or Notes:

DAY:_____

STAFF	EXHIBIT HOURS							

DAY:_____

STAFF	EXHIBIT HOURS							

DAY:_____

STAFF	EXHIBIT HOURS							

Work hours begin at 10 minutes before the hour and end 10 minutes after the hour.
Rest & Break periods begin 10 minutes after the hour and end 10 minutes before the hour

Show Services Check List:

	N/A	Ordered	Attached
Labor	☐	☐	☐
Rigger	☐	☐	☐
Carpet	☐	☐	☐
Electrical	☐	☐	☐
Water	☐	☐	☐
Gas	☐	☐	☐
Audio Visual	☐	☐	☐
Data recorder	☐	☐	☐
Computer	☐	☐	☐
Phone	☐	☐	☐
Internet	☐	☐	☐
Floral	☐	☐	☐
Food	☐	☐	☐
Beverage	☐	☐	☐
Temp Staff	☐	☐	☐
Entertainment	☐	☐	☐
Hospitality	☐	☐	☐
OTHER	☐	☐	☐
OTHER	☐	☐	☐
OTHER	☐	☐	☐
OTHER	☐	☐	☐

My Show Itinerary

CLIENT	Date/Time	Notes

COMPETITOR	Booth #	Date/Time	Focus

COMPLEMENTARY	Booth #	Date/Time	Focus

DISTRIBUTORS	Booth #	Date/Time	Focus

LEAD RETRIVAL FORM (sample)

Show Name	

Date		Sun	Mon	Tues	Wed	Thur	Fri	Sat

Name	

Title	

Address	

City	

Zip	

Phone	

Fax	

E-Mail	

Areas of Interest	1	2	3	4
	☐	☐	☐	☐
	☐	☐	☐	☐
	☐	☐	☐	☐
	☐	☐	☐	☐
	☐	☐	☐	☐
	☐	☐	☐	☐

Time Frame	Immediate	Intermediate	Long Range

Best Way To Contact	e-mail	phone	fax	mail	visit

NOTES:

Budgeting Worksheet

Trade show budget should be an investment not an expense.
The following worksheet lists common expense line items.
Keep an annual record for reporting Return on Investment
and to track profitability from year to year by show.

Line Item	Budget	Actual	Invoice #	Paid Date	Notes
Booth Space					
Current year					
Last year					
Deposit (next)					
Sub Total					
Structure					
Design					
Construction					
Refurbishment					
Staging					
Gang Box					
In & out fee					
Rental					
Storage*					
Insurance*					
Tax					
Sub Total					
Graphics					
Creation					
Acquisition					
Preparation					
Production					
Shipping					
Ground to					
Ground from					
Air to					
Air from					
Sea to					
Sea from					
Sub Total					

Line Item	Budget	Actual	Invoice #	Paid Date	Notes
Show services					
Audio Visual					
Bottled Water					
Carpet Rent					
Cleaning					
Computer Rent					
Signage					
Drayage in					
Drayage out					
Electrical					
Badges					
Floral/ Plant					
Furniture Rent					
Internet line					
Labor (I&D)					
Lead Retriever					
Photography					
Plumbing					
Riggers					
Safety Cont.					
Security					
Telephone					
Trash removal					
Sub Total					
Personnel					
Salaries					
Training					
Meetings					
Attire					
Transportation					
Hotel					
Parking					
Food					
Temporaries					
Entertainment					
Incentives					
Sub Total					
Promotion					
Ad print					
Ad radio					
Ad TV					
Creative					
Production					
Incentives					
Premiums					
Agency fees					

Line Item	Budget	Actual	Invoice #	Paid Date	Notes
Promo – cont.					
List rental					
Presenters					
Talent					
Media kits					
Press conf.					
Sponsorships					
Hospitality					
Discounts					
Postage					
Surveys					
Sub Total					
Lead Mgmt					
Form creation**					
Printing					
Postage					
Labor					
Equipment					
Software					
Sub Total					
Contingency***					
TOTAL					

* Insurance should be pro-rated based on allocated assets per show

** Form creation includes lead retrieval, cover letters and internal sales feedback forms.

*** Add 10% contingency for domestic, 15% international